Alcohol Awareness Workbook

by Jonathan Hussey and Jo Richardson

Published in 2013 by Bennion Kearny Limited.

Copyright © Bennion Kearny Ltd 2013

ISBN: 978-1-909125-26-1

Published by Bennion Kearny Limited
6 Victory House
64 Trafalgar Road
Birmingham
B13 8BU

www.BennionKearny.com

Cover image: © AirOne

About the Authors

Jonathan Hussey is one of the most exciting innovators of interventions for rehabilitating offenders today. He holds a B.Sc. (Hons) in Psychology from Loughborough University and a B.A. (Hons) in Community Justice Studies from Portsmouth University, as well as being a fully qualified, experienced, and award winning Probation Officer. Jonathan has worked extensively in the Criminal Justice System, but has specialised in leading roles within the Probation Service and Youth Offending Services. Jonathan currently works as a consultant for the Probation Service, and has established a successful training company; Intervention Consultancy (www.reoffending.org.uk).

Jo Richardson joined the Probation Service in 2005, initially within the Employment, Training and Education team before working as a Probation Officer from 2006. She works within a generic team managing offenders who pose a medium or high risk of serious harm to the public, including those within medium and high security mental health facilities, and of an extensive age range from young adults to elderly offenders. She is also trained as an Aggression Replacement Training (ART) facilitator, delivering this to both male and female offenders. Both her roles within the Probation Service have involved a high level of multi-agency working, including increasing the awareness of other agencies to the role of the Probation Service. Jo holds a BA (Hons) Community Justice Studies, Portsmouth.

Should you, or your organisation, require training on the delivery of these workbooks, then please contact Jonathan Hussey and Jo Richardson at interventioninfo@ymail.com

Table of Contents

Preface   **1**
The use of language   1
The purpose of this workbook   1
Who this workbook is for and the target client base   2
What this workbook covers   4
Delivering the Exercises   5

Section One   **7**
Cognitive Behavioural Therapy   7
The Cycle of Change   7
What are Cognitive Distortions and how can they be recognised?   10
What is Motivational Interviewing?   11
How to do Motivational Interviewing   12
What are learning styles? What are the factors to consider for each style?   14
Brief Intervention and Alcohol   15
The Principles of Brief Intervention (Alcohol)   16
Undertaking the Assessment for Brief Intervention   16
The 10 Steps to Doing a Successful Brief Assessment and Intervention   17
Bibliography   21

Section Two   **23**
Exercise 1 – The My Trigger Triangle   24
Exercise 2 – Decision Scale   33
Exercise 3 – Understanding Alcohol and Monitoring Use   44
Exercise 4 – Impact of Alcohol on Me   55
Exercise 5 – Alcohol and General Health   62
Exercise 6 – Impact of Alcohol on the Community   73
Exercise 7 – Alcohol and More on Health   85
Exercise 8 – Goal Setting   100
Exercise 9 – Changing General Behaviour   107

Exercise 10 – Dodge, Deal, Divert (DDD)   115
Exercise 11 – High Risk Situations   125
Exercise 12 – Final Exercise   132

Preface

How do you address an individual who commits crimes regularly when under the influence of alcohol? Do we just tell them what they did was wrong and to stop drinking alcohol? Or do we help the perpetrators of this crime come to an understanding themselves about the harm their behaviour and alcohol use has. Can we create either a progressive movement, or 'light bulb' moment, related to the harm they are causing, or which they have caused? Surely, if we believe people can change, then the latter will facilitate a better sustained change in an offender's behaviour? Developing this form of self-awareness is what this workbook sets out to achieve.

The use of language

In the following pages, this workbook will refer to the *facilitator, practitioner* or *tutor*. These terms mean the individual *delivering exercises* to the other person. These terms are interchanged, depending on the context, but they all mean the same thing here.

In turn, the following terms will refer to the person at whom the exercise is directed: *client*, *participant* and *offender*. Again these terms are interchanged, depending on the context.

The purpose of this workbook

The purpose of this workbook is to give the facilitator of any exercise an *easy-to-follow structure* to work from - with the client - to help build a basic level of self-awareness which will empower the client to reduce or stop their alcohol use and any related offending behaviour.

In order to build this motivation to change and increase awareness in the client, this workbook is specifically designed to help the client consider the negative effects of alcohol, the *consequences* of their actions, and also the *impact* it has on others.

To do this, the exercises in this workbook seek to help the client build a conscious recognition of the impact their behaviour has on both their own life, and the lives of those around them by using a strategy known as *brief intervention* (see section one).

Of course, this workbook does not claim that by completing the exercises the client will definitely achieve a reduction of alcohol use. However, if the facilitator can get the client to see the consequences of their alcohol use, it will hopefully act as an additional barrier to future problematic alcohol use or even offending behaviour.

As with all cognitive behavioural work, the majority of the exercises here are designed to create ambivalence (see section one) within the offender regarding their view as to the impact of their problematic behaviour – in this instance, alcohol misuse.

Who this workbook is for and the target client base

This workbook should be used on a one-to-one basis with the client. It should primarily be used by individuals who work with clients who have a link between alcohol misuse and offending or those who simply demonstrate problematic alcohol use. Examples of organisations that would benefit from this workbook includes professionals in the Probation and Prison Service. However, other professionals within schools and alcohol agencies may also benefit from the information contained in this workbook.

Note: All clients undertaking the exercises in this workbook should ideally undertake a questionnaire known as the *alcohol audit* which in itself can be found by visiting the World Health Organisation (WHO) website. Doing this will help the facilitator identify (with the client) how problematic the client's alcohol use is in relation to the population and also which form of intervention would best suit the client.

The targeted clients here should have, at the very least, a basic level of literacy and prove motivated to discuss their alcohol use. Those who fully deny their alcohol misuse, who say, for example: "I do not have a problem and do not want to talk about it" should not be considered suitable for the exercises in this workbook. Should the client, at a minimum, accept that there is some kind of problem or that 'maybe' their alcohol use is contributing to difficulties they are experiencing then they can be considered suitable.

It is worth recognising that many offenders may deny all, or parts, of their use. This is perfectly normal as many clients may use denial as a means of justifying, accepting, or coping with negative behaviour. Should you wish to learn more about addressing denial then look out for our separate workbook on this topic.

When considering working with offenders specifically, the exercises within this workbook are applicable to all offenders who have a link between alcohol misuse and offending.

Care must also be given to challenge 'inappropriate' answers, with enough time planned for each session to cover this. Inappropriate answers in this instance could be anything which indicates the offender is thinking of alcohol as controlling their behaviour or that they have 'no choice' but to drink. An example of this is when the client uses statements such as 'Alcohol *made me* act like that' or 'It's the [insert drink of choice] which makes me aggressive'.

Always be prepared to challenge inappropriate answers as they arise and in a motivational style (see section one). So, with this in mind, compare the brief conversations below and consider how this plays out in a session:

Practitioner: Let's talk about the link between your alcohol use and offending.

Offender: Again? It's not my fault, alcohol makes me act like that.

Practitioner: Well, that's an inappropriate comment. How can you say alcohol 'makes you'? It's your choice to drink and your choice to be aggressive once you have drunk.

Offender: I don't choose to be aggressive, I just told you – the alcohol makes me angry

Practitioner: Only you are in control of your actions. You're just using alcohol as an excuse to let you do what you want.

Offender: Argh! You're as bad as everyone else, you're just not listening to me. I'm not working with you. [Walks out]

Compare this to…

Practitioner: Let's talk about the link between your alcohol use and offending.

Offender: Again? It's not my fault, alcohol makes me act like that.

Practitioner: I'm not sure I follow you. Please explain more to me what you mean by the alcohol making you.

Offender: I'm only angry when I drink. Normally I'm known as the most chilled person but alcohol makes me lash out at stupid people.

Practitioner: Ok, so you're telling me that alcohol changes who you are. How much do you like the person that you become when you drink?

Offender: I'm still me when I drink, I just do different things. I like drinking but I'm not so keen on what I do when I'm drunk.

Practitioner: So if you're not a different person when you drink but you behave differently, are you telling me that alcohol controls you?

Offender: No!

Practitioner: Can I assume from that then, that you agree that only you control you?

Offender: Yes! I'm in charge of myself, thank you very much.

Practitioner: Can we just join those facts together then? You agree that only you control you but you also feel that you behave differently when you've been drinking. Right at the start, you told me that alcohol 'makes' that change in your behaviour. Explain that to me again please?

Offender: Ummm, I'd not looked at it like that before.

What this workbook covers

This workbook is divided into two main sections.

Section One

This section covers some of the basic theoretical knowledge needed by the facilitator to undertake the accompanying exercises. It covers: What is Cognitive Behavioural Therapy (CBT), The Cycle of Change, Motivational Interviewing, 'Thinking Errors', learning styles and understanding *brief intervention*. Following an exploration into what each element is, we will explain briefly, where possible, how to undertake each skill.

Note: Should the facilitator already know these skills, then they can simply begin the exercises.

Caution: Section one is primarily for the practitioner's reference and is not designed to be shared with the offender.

Section Two

Section two covers the workbook exercises themselves. Here we shall explain exercises that will help the client build up a basic understanding of the impact of their alcohol use and strategies to control or stop using alcohol.

Note: Generally, the exercises in section two are ideally to be used in sequence. However, where appropriate, the facilitator can use the exercises as standalone tasks depending on the assessed needs of the client. To help the practitioner undertake the exercises on a standalone basis, we have broken the exercises into two broad groups. These being: consequential thinking and general thinking skills. This should hopefully give the practitioner a quick reference as to whether any particular exercise is suitable for their client.

When assessing the client's needs, the facilitator must use their professional judgement as to where the client resides in the cycle of change (see section one) *and then* decide which exercises are relevant.

Delivering the Exercises

Prior to each exercise, the facilitator will see **Tutor Notes**. These will give a description or step-by-step guidance on how to run each exercise. The facilitator should read the notes and follow them. The subsequent worksheets for the client follow the Tutor Notes.

Now, regardless of whether the exercises are being delivered as a single session, or as a sequential programme, they should always be completed with a simple verbal 'summing-up' of what was covered at the end of each exercise.

Tip: the facilitator should never start a session without thinking carefully about, and planning for, examples of answers that the offender may offer. It may sound obvious but if the facilitator is stumped by a question then the exercise can lose its intended impact. This also helps prepare the facilitator to address potentially inappropriate or anti-social answers.

Lastly, when undertaking any exercise, the facilitator should never be afraid to use a *neutral* example from their own lives as an illustration of the types of answers that the exercise is attempting to draw out from the client. However, these examples should *not* be deeply personal – these exercises are for the client, not therapy for the facilitator, nor to place the facilitator at risk.

Out of Session Work (optional)

Following each exercise, and to offer more to the client - thus reinforcing learning - optional out of session work is also suggested. These out of session work exercises can be used if the practitioner feels that it would be beneficial for the offender. However, it is not a required part of proceedings.

Adapting the Sessions and Alternative Exercises

Recognising a client's *learning style* (see section one) is imperative for ensuring that the client really understands what is being put to them by the tutor. Therefore, within this workbook, we also offer an alternative way to deliver each exercise where possible.

Section One

Cognitive Behavioural Therapy

This workbook uses the theoretical basis of Cognitive Behavioural Therapy (CBT). Cognitive behaviourism as a whole, and in relation to working with offenders, works towards achieving a sense of personal responsibility within the offender for their behaviour and the resultant consequences (Chui, 2003:68-9). So, if the facilitator can motivate the offender to take responsibility for their behaviour and consider the consequences of their negative actions, then the offender may change their negative behaviours accordingly. But how does CBT enable the facilitator to do this?

CBT in itself is a form of therapy which aims to create an 'ability' in the person to address their problems. Unlike other therapies, it is rooted in the 'now' and looks at how our emotions colour how we approach any given situation. It also helps the client to understand how previous experiences may have shaped our current values and behaviour.

Through CBT, an offender can come to understand their own motives better, and challenge their problematic behaviour; replacing it with more pro social actions. In basic terms, the CBT approach believes that by changing someone's thinking, especially 'flawed' thinking, the resultant behaviour will also change. So, in keeping with the CBT approach, within this workbook, the exercises we propose will help the client consider the implications of their actions by changing their thinking.

The Cycle of Change

The *Cycle of Change* was developed by DiClemente and Prochaska as an aid to assist people in understanding why some people are able to make (and sustain changes) whilst others fail to recognise the need for change. It is also a model that provides a foundation for understanding the stages an individual 'progresses through' when trying to change their behaviour.

The Cycle of Change very simply breaks down the process of change into six areas defined by a person's motivation, and indeed ability, to change (Hussey 2012). We believe that it is critical that the facilitator understands the concept of the Cycle Of Change because one of the aims of this workbook is to increase the client's internal level of motivation to change by, at the very least, moving them firmly into the *contemplation phase* of this cycle, if not through to the *preparation phase*. So, what are these phases?

Using an offender as an example again, initially, a person may begin in a stage called *pre contemplation*, where there is no recognition of an existing problem. With offenders, this can be seen as a state of denial related to either the offence or the harm it has caused.

Through creating ambivalence towards an offender's current lifestyle, movement can be made towards *contemplation* where a person begins to identify drawbacks to their choices and starts to desire change.

The next stages are *preparation* (also known as *decision*) and *action*. *Preparation* to change and *action* are rather self-explanatory. These phases often occur in quick succession as the motivation brought about by a decision to change behaviour feeds into the actions to alter their behaviour in accordance with their newly desired decision(s). If progress through these stages is achieved, then the person can move forwards to *maintenance* (Fleet and Annison, 2003; Winstone and Hobbs, 2006:262-8).

Note: Should the client conclude in the decision phase that change is too difficult, or 'not worth the effort', this then results in a return to a state of *pre contemplation*.

Assuming that the client is now in a stage of *maintenance*, there is some debate about the next movement of the client. This debate centres around whether, having made a change, a person remains in the maintenance phase permanently, or whether he/she leaves the cycle when that change becomes internalised or a 'habit'.

As stated in Hussey (2012), for some to remain in the cycle forever is a rather depressing thought and so to aim to practice and perfect a change, to the point where exiting the cycle in a positive manner is achievable, can be a more encouraging viewpoint.

As mentioned above, the potential to exit the cycle at any stage through a lapse or relapse to old behaviours is always possible. A 'lapse' tends to refer to a momentary slip to previous behaviours, which can subsequently lead to either a return to the cycle or an exit from the cycle via a 'relapse' and the abandonment of change (Winstone and Hobbs, 2006:262-8).

For the visual learners amongst you, here is a diagram of the Cycle of Change:

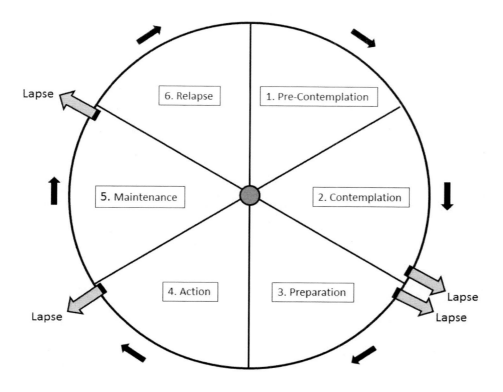

Lapse

Lapse

Lapse

Lapse

6. Relapse

1. Pre-Contemplation

5. Maintenance

2. Contemplation

4. Action

3. Preparation

How to use the Cycle of Change

Using an offender who has just been sentenced as an example, and anticipating that the offender who undertakes the exercises is at the beginning of their sentence, we will assume that they are in the pre contemplation stage (with a belief that they do not need to change) regarding their offending behaviour. Here, the practitioner would use their understanding of the Cycle of Change to create ambivalence within the offender concerning offending - in an attempt to move them to the next stage of contemplation. To do this, the practitioner should try to create doubt in the client about the validity and worthwhileness of the offending behaviour. The facilitator should also try to encourage the offender to (at least) entertain the idea that there are other options. This stage can very much be the 'drip drip' approach to eroding seemingly set ideas.

Once an offender has moved into the contemplation stage, where they are open to discussing and even admitting that their offending behaviour is harmful, more work can be undertaken to underpin this theoretical shift; in particular the way the offender views the world towards more concrete behavioural choices and actions. This period can be a very unnerving time for the offender because they are, in many ways, 'undoing' what they thought they knew. So if this happens, and they start to move back to pre contemplation, the facilitator should do their best to support the offender in considering new options and moving them to the decision stage where there is a conscious choice to change.

Note: See how the above says 'assist' and 'support' not *advise*. Advice is a very thorny topic; no one generally wants to be told what to do and even when it is given, accepted and acted upon, then it will probably not be a lasting change as it *was not that person's choice*. The practitioner is there to help the offender make new decisions, not tell them what they should be doing (no matter how tempting this may be) under the guise of 'advice'.

Once the offender has decided to change and puts their new thoughts into action, it is here that the facilitator should discuss with them the obstacles of maintaining their new path. The reason for this is not to be negative or to encourage them to fail, but to allow them to realise and accept how it is going to be a difficult transition and that they should not just give up at the first hurdle, or indeed lapse.

What are Cognitive Distortions ('thinking errors') and how are they recognised?

In order to move offenders forward within the Cycle of Change, this workbook seeks to explore the impact and consequences of the client's behaviour (with the client) on themselves and those around them. The exercises are designed to explore a client's thinking which, according to the trigger triangle (see Exercise 1) and CBT, will aid a change in behaviour.

 However, on occasion the client may make a comment which is known as a *Cognitive Distortion*. But what are cognitive distortions?

In brief, a cognitive distortion is a 'thinking error' (Hussey 2012). It is a particular way of looking at a fact, or part of life, which acts to overemphasise or exaggerate that issue, often leaving no alternative or way back once identified as 'fact'. For example, an offender may have decided that 'all the Police' hate them and therefore be unable to consider approaching authority for assistance. The fact that very few people are 'always' targeted by Police, and that all Police Officers will differ in their approach towards their treatment of offenders, and that each meeting with the Police is likely to be a different experience is too much detail for the distortion and as such these facts are dismissed by the offender's thinking error.

Sometimes, a cognitive distortion can be a comfortable way of thinking for an offender (or anyone for that matter) even if it is incredibly negative and damaging, because there are no subtleties or unknowns. Therefore change is difficult.

Cognitive distortions do not always lead to offending behaviour and examples of distortions can be found in most aspects of life. However, where distortions related to offending are identified, they can be key in understanding both why an offender chooses to behave in such a manner, and also how to address that behaviour. Using the 'trigger triangle', covered later, cognitive distortions provide an illustration of the possible thoughts which are feeding an individual's offending behaviour.

Cognitive distortions are typically associated with depressive thinking and there are many different types of cognitive distortions. Discussion of these is beyond this workbook. Knowledge of them can be gained from further reading and practitioners may find such additional reading useful. Should you want to read more on the types of thinking errors then a useful book in exploring these is the related book (written by one of this workbook's co-authors, Jonathan Hussey) entitled: *Reoffending: a practitioner's guide to addressing offending behaviour in the Criminal Justice System*.

A working example of a cognitive distortion from real life practice could be when an offender tells themselves: "I am a bad person" when, in fact, it is only part of their behaviour which is bad. They may, in fact, be a very pleasant person ninety-nine percent of the time and it is only one percent of the time when their behaviour can be seen as 'bad' or antisocial. This type of thinking error or cognitive distortion is called over-generalising. So, by highlighting the cognitive distortion to the offender, and breaking it down through exercises, the offender is given the opportunity to adjust their thinking and change their behaviour.

When considering the above, it is the internal dialogue which will enable an offender to move through the Cycle of Change and it is therefore envisaged that the practitioner will support alcohol awareness work with other offending behaviour work, as well as more holistic support, running concurrently.

What is Motivational Interviewing?

Motivational Interviewing (MI) is a method of working with offenders created by Miller and Rollnick (1991). Where other methods may build a relationship in which change can happen - MI provides a method of progressing and directing that change.

MI is a particular way of facilitating the recognition of problems and addressing them; motivation is a fluctuating state and MI uses a systematic strategy to build internal motivation to tackle these - rather than external pressure (Miller and Rollnick, 1991 cited in Fleet and Annison, 2003:133), linking it to normative compliance. Confrontation is an aim of, rather than a process of, MI (Winstone and Hobbs, 2006:259). However, it is important to note that this confrontation is not code for 'argument' with the offender. The confrontation regards their ideas and statements.

There are five key principles:

1. Being empathetic and accepting of the individual although not the behaviour
2. The development of discrepancies in an offender's cognitive distortions leading to the questioning of beliefs
3. The avoidance of argument through rolling with resistance
4. Seeing resistance as part of an offender's reaction to discomfort with the realisation of their cognitive distortions
5. Supporting efficacy through building belief in the offender's own abilities

(Fleet and Annison, 2003:133-6).

MI is often linked to the Cycle of Change as its principles can be integrated into the cycle. A substantial advantage to MI is that it can be delivered effectively in one session. MI also introduces protective factors which can be considered as reasons to sustain any changes made within a lifestyle. Ideally these protective factors would be internal beliefs rather than external, as the potential for an external factor to change or 'let down' the offender (if it were a person they were changing 'for', for example) can create the potential for lapse (Winstone and Hobbs, 2006:284). It is worth noting, however, that female offenders may pick an external factor such as their child and that this could be linked to social bond theory considerations such that family responsibilities are likely to cause desistance in female offenders (Rex, 1999:374).

As with any approach, there are no guarantees for success; an offender may exit the Cycle of Change by decision if they determine that they are content with their current lifestyle and the process of using MI would need to begin again.

How to do Motivational Interviewing

MI involves being able to direct a conversation with a person so that they are able to discover a truth for themselves. The practitioner needs to be able to read the feedback from the person sat with them in the form of both verbal and non-verbal communication. Listening to what the person is trying to say and reflecting this back to them, either to highlight a discrepancy with their statements or to enable them to find the meaning, are crucial skills. Unhelpful statements are those that contain advice, threats, criticism or direct commands - however tempting.

During any one session, several things are important; being specific in the feedback that is given to the offender (especially praise), listening carefully to the client, using both summarising and reflective listening to prove that the client has been heard, making sure questions are open questions, and encouraging self-motivating questions. These are all evidence that MI is in use.

If the offender resists or is disruptive then change the practice approach, do not attempt to force them to change, this is known as rolling with resistance.

An example discussion using MI:

Practitioner: Thank you for being punctual. I've noticed that you've been on time the last two sessions. Today we need to look at your index offence and why it's been linked to your alcohol use.

Offender: This is getting really annoying; I've only got an 'alcohol problem' because you say I do.

Practitioner: Are you telling me that you believe there are no difficulties at all associated with your alcohol use?

Offender: That's not what I said.

Practitioner: Explain to me what you meant?

Offender: It's not drinking the alcohol that's a problem. I've not had much money since I got booted out of my last job and it's not fair that I can't go out with my friends. If someone is stupid enough to make it easy for me to take the odd bit of money or bottle, then I will. It's not hurting anyone.

Practitioner: That's a lot of information you just told me. Let's break it down a bit. Tell me why you lost your last job?

Offender: I turned up with a hangover and the idiot of a foreman told me it was 'unacceptable'.

Practitioner: So you'd gone out drinking on an evening when you had to be at work the next day. And your employer felt that it wasn't safe for you to be working when you might not be fully sober yet?

Offender: Oh seriously, get off my case. You sound like my parents.

Practitioner: Ok. Let's look at the next bit you told me. You said that you felt left out by your friends; that you couldn't always afford to go out with them. Also, you feel that it's you that gets identified within the group as having the most negative behaviour when you've all been drinking. Tell me a bit more about that.

Offender: What else is there to say? You've just said it all.

Practitioner: If you agree with me, tell me why you think those facts are true.

Offender: Well, when I do finally actually get to go out with my mates, I want it to be a time to remember as it'll be ages before I get to go again. Besides, I'm known as the mad one when we go out; I'm always up for it.

Practitioner: Can I understand from that, that you maybe drink a bit more than the others, to make the most of the opportunity and to make sure you're fun enough to be invited out again?

Offender: Yeah. Umm, I'd not put it that way before.

Practitioner: Thinking again about why you feel I've labelled 'alcohol use' as a problem… can you think of any reasons for this?

Offender: Alright, alright. Maybe every time I get in trouble I've used alcohol at some point. I'm not saying you're right though.

What are learning styles? What are the factors to consider for each style?

We do not all learn in the same manner, and learning styles are a way of recognising this. There are three main recognised ways in which we learn:

Auditory: where preference is given to listening to relayed information through lectures or discussions.

Visual: where a person is best able to take in information they can 'see' in the form of presentations, books and diagrams.

Kinaesthetic: where learners prefer to 'do' in order to learn for themselves.

Evidence has shown that offenders tend to be kinaesthetic learners, requiring a participatory approach rather than a didactic one (Hopkinson and Rex, 2003:165) and this is worth bearing in mind when considering the manner in which to deliver an exercise, or whether it needs to be broken down over several sessions. There are various questionnaires available which can be completed with an offender to determine the best style of learning for them. However, caution should be exercised when labelling an offender as having a particular style. It is only a guide and not a necessity to subsequently present all information rigidly in that manner.

This workbook provides some examples of presenting the same exercise in different styles, however almost any exercise can be adapted. It doesn't have to be a complex process to change information from a diagram to spoken or as an 'experiment'. Below are three ways of presenting the same information regarding an offender's sentence:

Auditory Simply stating: "You were sentenced to three years in custody. You've now served half of that in prison and so been released. You will spend the rest of your sentence on licence. Part of that licence is to report weekly to Probation for supervision where we will undertake work to address issues related to your offending. If you fail to attend these appointments, or break any other conditions of release, such as committing another offence, then you may be recalled to prison."

Visual

Kinaesthetic Chop the above diagram into pieces and ask the offender to reassemble the diagram (like a jigsaw) with discussion as to why they think pieces go in certain places.

Brief Intervention and Alcohol

As stated previously, this workbook is based on the work developed by the World Health Organisation (WHO) called *brief intervention*.

Brief intervention is a highly effective tool that is an 'assessment and personalised discussion' of a client's alcohol consumption level, and how it relates to the general population. It can be so adaptive that it can range from a five minute meeting to several sessions depending on the need of the client, with its primary function being to supply advice on reducing alcohol consumption in a persuasive but non-judgemental way.

The Principles of Brief Intervention (Alcohol)

Brief intervention is fundamentally about getting an understanding (as accurately as possible) of an individual's alcohol misuse while all the time trying to get the client to 'think' about the problems their use may cause and then assisting them in minimising the risks associated with their alcohol use.

When the facilitator is discussing the *risks* of alcohol use with the client, this not only relates to risks to the client, but also a consideration of the harm caused to others.

Tip: Remember that when professionals undertake brief interventions, they are attempting to minimise, not remove, alcohol use in the safest possible way.

In order to undertake brief interventions, the practitioner should recognise the following principles:

1. Start by undertaking an assessment of the problem. This can be through a simple questionnaire which is called an alcohol audit.
2. Continuously, as a practitioner, be non-judgemental and place an emphasis on personal choice and personal responsibility. Give the client ownership of the problem; change will be their decision not yours.
3. Give non-judgemental support on *how* the client could change their behaviour and offer them a number of different options. This includes assisting them in how to achieve these options through goal setting exercises (as discussed in section two).
4. Critically, be empathetic not sympathetic. Try to recognise the problem from the client's standpoint but note and continually remind yourself that this does not necessarily involve agreeing with them.

Undertaking the Assessment for Brief Intervention

In many situations, practitioners are faced with a client who does not want to change or who does not recognise that they have a problem. How can this be tackled?

Firstly, as stated in the principles of brief intervention above, adopt a non-judgmental position, try to put yourself in the client's shoes, and see things the way they see them.

Then help the client see how their current behaviour is not conducive to achieving their long term goals; this is achieved through motivational interviewing as described previously. If a practitioner does not take the time to first understand a client's perspective, then how can that client be expected to attempt to look at the situation differently?

Warning: do not be overly sympathetic with an offender's situation as this may lead to collusion. Empathy involves understanding (not agreeing with) the feelings of another person and it allows for a gentle challenging of problematic thinking and behaviour.

Below is a set of ten steps as a guide of how to implement a brief intervention, focussing on a first session. Note that we believe this should be undertaken on a one to one basis due to the personal and private nature of the work; and also because the client is being expected to be extremely honest and having additional people around may simply create additional barriers to this honesty.

The 10 Steps to Doing a Successful Brief Assessment and Intervention

These steps are set out to be similar to the exercises in section two of this workbook.

Step 1: Explain to the client that you would like to do a brief assessment with them to look at their drinking patterns. Explain that this is a short process that requires them to be as honest as possible. State that should they not tell you the truth, then in reality they are only cheating themselves as it's likely to lead them to a treatment that will not work for them.

This should set the scene or contract for the session. It also promotes honesty and openness which is important for the working relationship. For more detail on creating a good working relationship, see the related book to this workbook *Reoffending: A practitioner's guide to working with offenders and offending behaviour in the Criminal Justice System.*

Step 2: With the client, complete what is known as an alcohol audit questionnaire (as discussed earlier). This questionnaire asks a series of questions and offers the client a series of possible answers (multiple choice). Each answer generates a static score. Often the client will automatically guess that the higher the score the more problematic their use is - and so they will be tempted to hide the truth. Therefore reassure the client before you start: "Do not worry about the score here, just answer everything as honestly as possible."

By doing this you are, at the very least, making an attempt to look after the quality and validity of the data obtained.

Step 3: If the client is able, ask *them* to add the final scores together, in order to foster the sense of ownership which is critical to the change process. If they cannot do this, help them but work through it together. One way to do this is to simply ask questions such as: "Four plus two equals six, right?" or something to that effect.

Step 4: Once a total score is generated circle it and tell the client: "Right, this is your score, and this is personal to you."

In order to set some context for discussing scores, below are some score ranges for an example alcohol audit questionnaire. The actual values are not important here (and the scoring system/range will vary between different questionnaires), it is the relative spectrum of drinking misuse, and where people fall, that should be noted:

• LOW: A score between 0-7 indicates either Low Risk Drinkers or non-drinkers. Within this area, there is probably no need for an intervention. These individuals usually consume alcohol to a limited degree, or not at all, and their use is not seen as problematic.

• MEDIUM: A score between 8-14 falls within the area of Hazardous Drinkers. This is usually associated with binge drinkers, which according to the WHO are those that consume more than six alcoholic drinks in one sitting, although the definition varies widely. The NHS states that a 'binge' is defined by drinking more than double the daily recommended alcohol intake in one session. An example here would be the stereotypical image of a university student drinker.

• MEDIUM HIGH: A score between 15-21 enters the area of Harmful Drinkers. Here alcohol users usually have some form or problematic pattern of drinking that will be damaging to them. An example would be an individual who begins to drink on an almost daily basis to excess, above the daily recommended intake of units, and fails to recognise the harm being caused to their health and life. However, in contrast, it is becoming even more frequent to find that some individuals who fall in this bracket can function to a high level in extremely difficult roles (such as lawyers, doctors) and no one other than those close to them will recognise that a problem is developing.

• HIGH: A score between 22-30 indicates a Moderately Dependant Drinker. Such a score is a significant warning sign to the practitioner; a referral to a specialist agency should be made immediately. Those who fall within this bracket have often developed or are developing significant health problems. Their lifestyle may also be relatively problematic resulting in regular offending behaviour.

• VERY HIGH: And finally, 31-40 indicates Severely Dependant Drinkers. Those who fall within this bracket will most likely have significant health problems already, and they may see alcohol as the main focal point of their life. Individuals here will often seek whatever possible opportunity to obtain and consume alcohol on a daily basis.

Step 5: Before examining the score with the client - reiterate the purpose of the questionnaire and where it comes from. Explain that the questionnaire is used by professionals in this field to give an assessment of how drinking levels compare to disclosed use within the population of the UK. Add that it gives us an idea of what treatment route will be most suitable and maybe help the client to see the score as just a number rather than a judgement or label.

Step 6: Explain that a score above the threshold score of the questionnaire usually indicates that the client will need to address their alcohol use in some way.

Tip: Ensure that you do not allow the client to see the threshold score, as it is usually written somewhere on the questionnaire. This is because, on occasion, the client may feel that if they are at the 'lower end' of the scoring system then they do not have as big a problem as their representative category suggests. This justification can then be used by the client to give themselves permission to continue with their current level of alcohol use.

Step 7: Discuss how the client feels about the score for a short period of time. It will usually shock a majority of people, but take time to explain that this score does not define them as a person, nor is it a label. Also, keep away from the phrase 'alcoholic'. Labelling a person is very powerful if they take on this identity. For example, If someone takes on and accepts the identity of the label of 'alcoholic' and states accordingly that there is "nothing they can do about it," ask yourself - how is this conducive to positive change?

Tip: It is worth recognising that the removal of labelling in this system of brief intervention is in stark contrast to that of Alcoholics Anonymous (AA). With AA it is the use of a label (in part) that is employed in order to clearly identify the problem at hand.

Step 8: Now reflect on the score with the client and how it compares to the rest of the population. Some of the more critical clients may ask further questions in relation to the validity of the questionnaire. It is important here that you highlight how the questionnaire is just a method used to give an idea of use and possible treatments. If you have a particularly inquisitive client, simply direct them to the WHO, National Health Service, or Drink Aware websites (see bibliography).

Step 9: Returning to what was started in Step 7, continue the discussion with regards to how the individual *feels* about the results. It is important to have a definition to hand of what each category means. This can be obtained from the World Health Organisation website.

Step 10: Finally, give some basic advice on safeguarding the user. This should include discussing the consequences of continued use to them, and society around them. Look at possible treatment options and try to motivate the user to engage with the appropriate agency.

It is not within the remit of this workbook to give a comprehensive account of how to undertake this style of intervention with alcohol abuse as a whole. When reflecting on categories of alcohol use, this workbook is designed primarily to be used with those clients that fall into the hazardous and harmful drinker types. Those falling into the moderately dependant and severely dependent categories need to be treated by specialist agencies. However, this does not rule out providing support through a brief intervention prior to the start of specialist treatment, especially to motivate that person to undertake the treatment.

Some Useful Tips:

Tip 1: When discussing the impact of falling into a specific drinking type, try using a cost/benefit analysis, which is described in exercise 2. This attempts to motivate the user to reflect on the pros and cons of continued drinking in their present manner. The aim here is to move the client from wavering pre-contemplation to firm contemplation, or if they are in contemplation to decision and action (Cycle of Change).

Tip 2: Always seek to explore how to achieve any goals generated during the session. Make sure this goal setting is realistic and achievable.

Tip 3: It may be a good idea to be as creative as possible with this intervention. Look at the client's learning style(s) and incorporate them into the session. This could include the use of videos, visual aids, role play, or even just discussions. The great thing about brief interventions is that, as long as the practitioner sticks to the principles, the actual implementation can be as creative as appropriate.

Bibliography

Chui, W. H. (2003) What Works in Reducing Re-Offending: Principles and Programmes. In W. H. Chui and M. Nellis (Eds.) *Moving Probation Forwards: Evidence, Arguments and Practice*. pp56-70, Pearson Longman: Essex

Farrell S. and Maltby, S. (2003) The Victimisation of Probationers. *The Howard Journal*, 42(1), 32-54

Fleet, F. and Annison, J. (2003) In Support of Effectiveness: Facilitating Participation and Sustaining Change. In W. H. Chui and M. Nellis (Eds.) *Moving Probation Forwards: Evidence, Arguments and Practice*. pp129-143, Pearson Longman: Essex

Gilchrist, E. and Blissett, J. (2002) Magistrates' Attitudes to Domestic Violence and Sentencing Options. *The Howard Journal*, 41(4), 348-363

Hussey, J. (2012) *Reoffending: A practitioners Guide to Working With Offenders and Offending Behaviour in the Criminal Justice System*. Bennion Kearny: Birmingham

Ministry of Justice (2010) *Breaking the Cycle: Effective Punishment, Rehabilitation and Sentencing of Offenders*. HMSO: London

Rex, S. (1999) Desistance from Offending: Experiences of Probation, *The Howard Journal*, 38(4), 366-383

Spalek, B. (2003) Victim Work in the Probation Service: Perpetuating Notions of an Ideal Victim. In W.H. Chui and M. Nellis (Eds.) *Moving Probation Forwards. Evidence, Arguments and Practice*. pp.215-225 Pearson Longman: Harlow

Walklate, S. (2004) *Gender, Crime and Criminal Justice (2nd ed.)* Willan: Devon

Winstone, J. and Hobbs, S. (2006) *Strategies for Tackling Offending Behaviour, Volume 2*. 231-395, University of Portsmouth: Portsmouth

http://www.drinkaware.co.uk/understand-your-drinking/is-your-drinking-a-problem/binge-drinking

http://www.who.int/bulletin/volumes/88/9/10-010910/en/index.html

Section 2

The Exercises

Despite our use of the term "offender", as discussed in section one of this workbook, this by no means excludes other individuals who misuse alcohol. However, this workbook is ideal as a form of intervention for a young person who regularly binge drinks or as a form of early intervention for adults.

The exercises have been written with a target audience of both male and female clients, aged fifteen and older. However, should a practitioner feel that a younger person would benefit from this workbook, care would need to be taken to ensure the language used and examples within exercises are appropriate.

At the end of any exercise, the facilitator should ask the client what they have learned from that exercise. The answer should then be written onto the worksheet. The reason for this is that once the facilitator has completed all the exercises they want to use with the client, the learning points (which are personal to the client) can be summarised and fed back to the client, in keeping with the MI style of working (see section one).

Exercise 1 – The My Trigger Triangle

Category of exercise: General thinking skills.

Tutor Notes

The Cognitive Behavioural Therapy (CBT) Triangle is an important element which, for the purposes of this workbook, should be explored first by the tutor with the offender. So, to undertake this exercise, the tutor will need to know what the CBT Triangle is within the context of this workbook.

Here, the CBT Triangle demonstrates and emphasises the link that all behaviour is preceded by a thought and feeling. It is also represented in the diagrammatic form of a triangle (see worksheet).

Why is it important? The tutor's aim is to get the client to become consciously aware, and in control, of the thoughts and feelings they have *before* any given action, in this case using alcohol. Here, the idea is that if a client can control their thoughts and feelings, then they can change their behaviour/alcohol use. So, for example, if the client develops a more holistic understanding (thoughts and feelings) of the harm alcohol can have, then they may decide to rethink the way in which they use alcohol.

In this workbook, the CBT Triangle is re-named as *My Trigger Triangle*. The purpose of this is to give it a more personal feel to the offender. It is hoped that once the offender understands this exercise they can begin to 'own' their behaviour (take responsibility) as they become more consciously aware of their thoughts and feelings.

Step 1: Explain to the client that: "This triangle forms the basis of *all* the work that you will be doing." Here it is a good idea for the tutor to explain a little about why it is important. You can use the explanation in the tutor notes should you wish.

Step 2: Show the client the Trigger Triangle diagram.

Step 3: Explain to the client that:

- Behaviour can always be controlled and is heavily affected by our thoughts and feelings.
- If we can change any element of this triangle, then we can change all the other parts too.

Step 4: Explain that before we explore this further, we will first look to *define* what thoughts, feelings and behaviour are.

Tip: Do not look to over-complicate this definition exercise but ensure that there is clarity on (at least) a very basic level of understanding. For example, simply seek to clarify the definitions as follows:

Thoughts: The things we think about in our mind; e.g. "I need a drink."

Feelings: The things we feel inside; e.g. "sad, happy, angry".

Behaviour: An action, the physical part of the triangle that can be seen by others; e.g. *picking up* a pint glass.

Tip: It is important that the client understands the difference between thoughts and feelings. For example, "I am feeling sad" is a thought about a feeling, not a feeling in itself.

Step 5: Show the client the '*My Trigger Triangle*' diagram once again and ask the client to write under the headings, using their offence or a recent problematic incident as the example of behaviour, what thoughts and feelings they had before it happened.

Tip: If the offender is particularly resistant to exploring their offence in this manner, at this time, then 'roll with the resistance' and allow them to pick another example to use. However, do make sure that the offence is revisited before the completion of the 'treatment' and a trigger triangle completed for it.

Step 6: Conclude the exercise by explaining what was originally set out in the exercise. This being: *all behaviour is preceded by a thought and feeling and if we can change our thoughts and feelings then we can change our actions.*

Tip: Here you may have to check that the client understands by asking them to give a further example to summarise what has been explored.

Exercise 1 – Worksheet

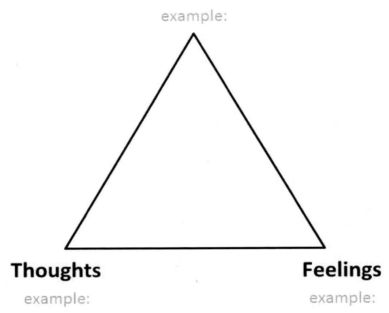

Behaviour
example:

Thoughts
example:

Feelings
example:

What is a Thought? Give an example of a thought you have about drinking alcohol:

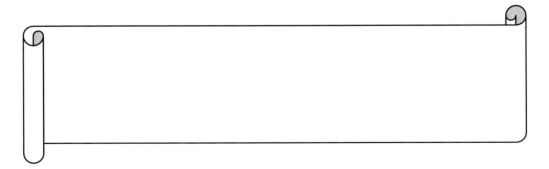

What is a Feeling? Give an example of a feeling you have about drinking alcohol:

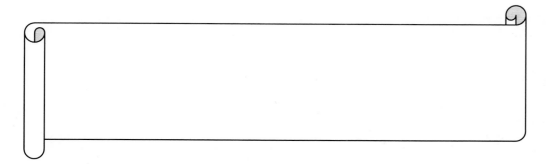

What is Behaviour? Give an example of an action or behaviour that you tend to do when under the influence of alcohol:

Exercise 1a – Alternative Exercise

Step 1: Prepare nine flashcards with pictures depicting a feeling, emotion or behaviour; three of each of these.

Step 2: Ask the offender to sort them into three piles of 'feelings', 'thoughts' and 'behaviour'. Discuss their choices and provide guidance where appropriate.

Step 3: Ask the offender to arrange the cards on the trigger triangle at the appropriate point, depending on whether the card is depicting a thought, feeling or behaviour, so that a sequence is created relating to one particular event.

Step 4: To check understanding, ask the offender to draw three pictures on the blank cards to create their own set of 'feeling, behaviour and thought' cards based on a behaviour they do regularly. An easy one would be 'eating' – a feeling of hunger, a thought of wanting a takeaway, and a behaviour of ordering one.

Exercise 1a – Worksheet

(angry)	(happy)	(love)
I want to kick it	I want a drink	Let's celebrate with Champagne
Feeling	Thought	Behaviour

Exercise 1 – Out of Session Work

Should the tutor feel that more work on this is needed then they can present some optional work to be completed by the client outside the session.

Step 1: Ask the client to complete a '*My Trigger Triangle*' for as many different situations as appropriate.

Step 2: Provide blank copies of the triangle and ask the offender to list - below the headings of thoughts, feelings, and behaviour - relevant examples for a specific situation that they have encountered in the week between sessions.

Tip: Generally, when this is completed, the wider the range of situations, the better the understanding of the triangle.

Exercise 1 – Out of Session Worksheet

Give an example of when a thought and feeling made you act in a specific way:

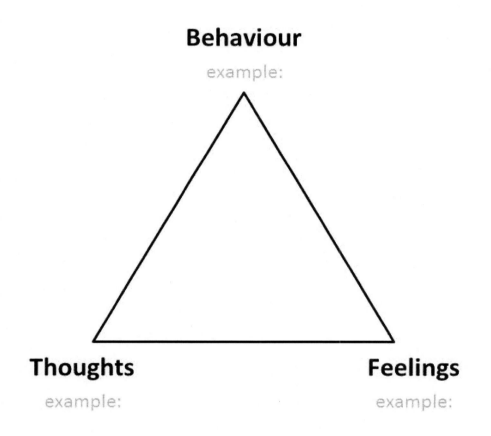

Exercise 1 – Review

Name at least one thing that has been learned from this exercise.

Additional Notes:

Exercise 2 – Decision Scale

Category of exercise: General thinking skills.

> **Tutor Notes**
>
> In this exercise, the practitioner's aim is to introduce the client to the general thinking skill of how to make an informed decision in relation to using alcohol. This is simply undertaken by looking at the positives and negatives of using alcohol, as in the following exercise.

Step 1: Explain to the client that: "Generally, people do the things they want to - for a particular given reason." With this in mind: "People consume alcohol because they want to, or choose to."

Step 2: Tell the client that: "If we want to act in a certain way, we do so because we tell ourselves that there is some benefit from doing so." So if we can control this form of "talking to oneself" we can control our behaviours – just as explained in *Exercise 1* (if this has been used).

Step 3: Explain to the client that one way to control our thoughts is to come up with *evidence* that the decision we are about to make is either a good or bad idea. For example: 'To drink or not to drink?'

Step 4: Explain that: "One tool we can use to help decide if an option is a good or bad decision is a *decision scale.*"

Note: This is actually an exercise formally known as a *cost benefit analysis*. The name has been changed here to simplify the exercise.

Step 5: Show the client the decision scale and ask the client to consider all the positives elements of drinking alcohol. List all the positives that the client comes up with. The facilitator should note here that *no answer is wrong*. This is important, as the client's answers are very individualistic to that person.

Note: Both the practitioner and the offender need to be able to accept that there are, and must be, positives to using alcohol. Otherwise we simply wouldn't do it.

Step 6: Ask the client to list all the negatives of drinking alcohol. Again the facilitator should promote responses by indicating that no answer is wrong. The facilitator should also ask the client to consider areas such as health, finances, relationships, etc. If the client is really struggling then they can use the fact that they are having to spend time looking at their alcohol use as a negative factor.

Step 7: Now ask the client to visualise a set of balanced weight scales. Ask the client to draw a horizontal line on the *balanced scales* across the apex of the triangle, to demonstrate the balanced nature of the scales visually on the worksheet. Use the top set of scales on the worksheet labelled 'balanced scales' for this part of the exercise.

Step 8: Now ask the client to consider that the answers they gave (in steps 5 and 6) can be thought of as weights to be placed on the scales. Here the facilitator should ask the client to draw the scales as to how they would look if they were able to put these 'weights' on the scales. Do the positive factors amount to a heavier or lighter load than the negatives? Ask the client to redraw the horizontal line onto the *my scales* set of scales with the correct orientation downwards for either the positive or negative side, depending on the given answers.

Tip: It is not about the number of facts for each side of the balance scales. One single fact may 'weigh' more heavily than another. For example the offender may feel that the only negative they were able to identify ("losing my family") is worth more weight than all the positives they identified. This is fine; simply allow the balance line to be drawn to reflect this.

Step 9: Ask the client something to the effect of: "Do the negatives of your drinking outweigh the positives?" Then discuss the responses with the client. Also, ask the client to write something they have learned and can take away from the session at the bottom of the worksheet.

Note: If a client feels that the positives of alcohol use outweigh the negatives, this is not necessarily an 'end game' for the intervention. What it shows the practitioner is how the offender feels about their drinking and therefore at what level to start and base the intervention. Roll with the resistance (see section one) and work with the offender over different sessions to challenge their attitude towards alcohol.

Exercise 2 – Worksheet

Is it really worth it? chart

Positives of Drinking Alcohol	Negatives of Drinking Alcohol

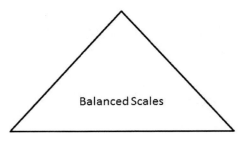

Balanced Scales

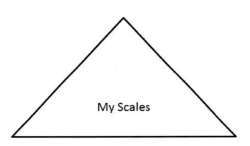

My Scales

What have you learned from this session?

Exercise 2a – Alternative Exercise

For the kinaesthetic and visual learners the following exercise is a great alternative, but it does require the facilitator to do a little work beforehand.

Step 1: Cut out all the "sometimes" statements in the accompanying worksheet.

Step 2: Shuffle the sometimes statements and read out each statement deciding, together with the client, if each statement is relevant and where it could go on the worksheet's scales. If a statement is thought to be relevant, place it on top of the line.

Step 3: Ask the client if they have any additional statements they would like to give, or comment on, about the effect that alcohol sometimes has on them. Write these on the blank statements then place the answers on the scales.

Step 4: The facilitator should ask the client to count how many negatives statements there are and how many positive statements there are. Following this, discuss whether it is a good decision or not to drink alcohol.

Tip: As per the tip detailed in Exercise 2 (above) it is not about the number of facts for each side of the balance scales. One single fact may 'weigh' more heavily than another.

Step 5: At the end of the session, ask the client to consider the learning points of the exercise and then complete the review section.

Exercise 2 – Worksheet

I can sometimes forget my problems when I drink alcohol	I sometimes have less money after I drink alcohol	Alcohol sometimes helps me socialise	Alcohol sometimes gives me confidence
Sometimes I lose control of my emotions when I drink alcohol	Sometimes I am happier when I drink alcohol	Sometimes alcohol has a bad effect on my relationship/s	Sometimes I become sad when I drink alcohol
Sometimes I struggle to get up the next day after I drink alcohol to excess	Sometimes I can get angry easily when I drink alcohol	Sometimes I like to drink alcohol	Sometimes I do not really like to drink alcohol but do it anyway
Sometimes alcohol affects my liver badly	Sometime alcohol causes me to be sick	Sometimes alcohol makes me feel not in control of my body	Sometimes I have caused someone harm when drinking alcohol

Alcohol sometimes damages my heart	Sometimes alcohol ...	Sometimes alcohol ...	Sometimes alcohol ...
Sometimes alcohol ...	Sometimes alcohol ...	Sometimes alcohol ...	Sometimes alcohol ...

Exercise 2 – Out of Session Work

Should the facilitator be of the view that the client would benefit from further exploration of this skill area, then the facilitator can of course provide out of session work.

The idea of Exercise 2 is to enable the client to 'weigh up' each side of an argument in their head and be able to then apply this to varying situations - hopefully and especially the ones that lead them to offend. This skill also requires being able to view situations from another perspective, even if they don't agree with it, in order to generate new ideas. The suggested out of session work is therefore a game of 'devil's advocate'.

Step 1: Run through the exercise steps below, before the end of the session, to ensure that the client fully understands matters.

Step 2: Explain that a devil's advocate is a colloquial term to describe someone who always argues the other side of what someone is saying, regardless of the situation or their own view.

Step 3: Read through the worksheet together and ask the offender to complete it prior to the next session, completing the empty boxes and adding more arguments to the completed side.

Step 4: Explain that the blank boxes are there to provide space for the offender's own examples, if they find any during the time between sessions.

Exercise 2 – Out of Session Worksheet

Statement	For	Against
Footballers are overpaid.	They earn more than most people earn, for a few games a month. It doesn't require that much talent to play.	
Prisons in the UK are 'soft'.		Deprivation of liberty (being locked up) is a powerful punishment. Sharing a cell with a stranger is not nice. People who say prisons are soft tend to have not experienced prison.
Alien and UFO conspiracy theories are true	It's crazy to think we are the only highly evolved forms of life in the universe.	The government doesn't have the resources to 'cover up' that much evidence.

Statement	For	Against

42

Exercise 2 – Review

Name at least one thing that has been learned from this exercise.

Additional Notes:

Exercise 3 – Understanding Alcohol and Monitoring Use

Category of exercise: Consequential thinking.

Tutor Notes

In this exercise, the tutor will explore with the client how much alcohol the client actually consumes whilst also touching upon 'why' they use. Following this, the exercise will begin to attempt to motivate the client to change by educating them about government recommendations.

Step 1: Explain to the client that one way to monitor how much alcohol we consume is by understanding the concept of *units* of alcohol.

Step 2: Explain that one way to keep on top of how much alcohol we consume is by using a drink diary. This is provided in the accompanying worksheet along with a guide as to how many units can be found in specific alcoholic drinks.

Step 3: The facilitator works with the client to consider how many units of alcohol they have used over the last week by filling in the diary (using the unit table as a guide). When finished, the client should also list all the reasons as to why they drank during that week (in the space provided) and with whom.

Step 4: Explain that the government recommends that men do not drink more than 3-4 units *regularly* and women no more than 2-3 units.

Step 5: Explain to the client that regular drinking means drinking every day or most days of the week.

Tip: Do not preach – guide the conversation towards healthy answers but do not judge or force a client to think their drinking habits are 'wrong'; this is a conclusion they must reach themselves. The job of a practitioner is to help a client reach that conclusion and then support them once they are there.

Exercise 3 – Worksheet

 A pint of lager on average is around 2.8 Units (5%)

 A large glass of wine on average is around 3.5 Units (250ml)

 A pint of cider on average is around 3.4 Units (6%)

 A pub shot of spirits is on average is around 1 Unit (25ml) (home measures are invariably larger)

 An alcopop is on average around 1.5 Units.

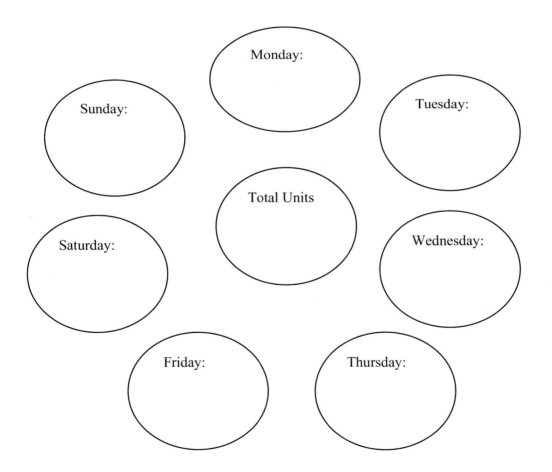

List all your reasons why you drink alcohol:

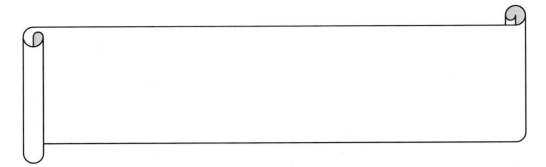

Circle the answer which best fits whom you drink with:

Monday: Alone / with others / bit of both

Tuesday: Alone / with others / bit of both

Wednesday: Alone / with others / bit of both

Thursday: Alone / with others / bit of both

Friday: Alone / with others / bit of both

Saturday: Alone / with others / bit of both

Sunday: Alone / with others / bit of both

How many units can I have?

The government advises that men should not consume more than 3-4 units of alcohol and women 2-3 units on a regular basis.

Regular Drinking: *Drinking every day or most days of the week.*

What thoughts do you have about this?

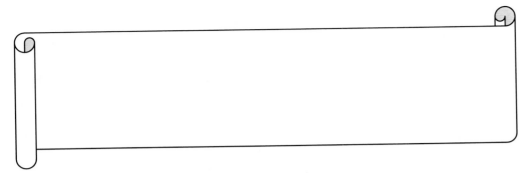

What feelings do you have about this?

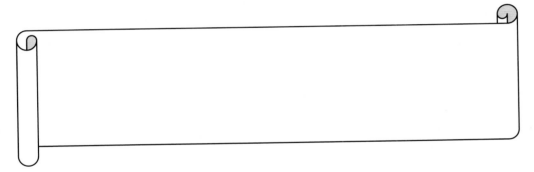

When considering who you drink with; what thoughts and feelings do you have about drinking alone or with others?

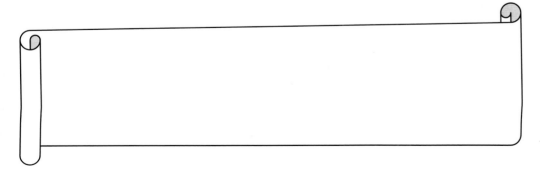

Exercise 3a – Alternative Exercise

This exercise requires prior preparation from the facilitator.

Before the session, take five glasses (if there are safety concerns use plastic glasses but they must be transparent), and label them 'wine', 'whisky', 'alcopop', 'beer', and 'cider'. Fill them with the relevant volume of fluid (water) for each measure (so a pint of beer and cider, 170ml of wine, etc.) If you have time, colour them with the relevant colour using food colouring.

Step 1: Cut out the cards on the accompanying worksheet. In this exercise, each card represents one unit of alcohol.

Step 2: Ask the client to place in front of each of the 'drinks' how many units they think that the glass contains. Once this is completed, in a separate column next to the client's guess, lay out the actual number of cards/units (the units are referenced on the worksheet. Where there is a decimal point in the units contained, simply fold or rip the unit square to represent this). Discuss any differences with the client.

Step 3: Next, ask the client to try to remember how much they have drunk during the last week. For each alcoholic drink they recall, the tutor should give the client the appropriate number of cards.

Step 4: Once the client has got all their cards for the week, the tutor should ask the client how many cards they think the government advises they have on a regular basis.

Step 5: Once the answer has been disclosed, the tutor takes away the client's cards until they are left with the recommended number of cards (based on the government's advice). Spread the removed cards out on the table and ask the client to keep hold of the 'allowed' ones.

Step 6: Ask the client what their thoughts and feelings are about this. Look at whether they are shocked or whether they suspected they were drinking over the recommended amount. What are their feelings about the level of alcohol consumption that is recommended?

Exercise 3a – Worksheet

 A pint of lager on average is around 2.8 Units (5%)

 A large glass of wine on average is around 3.5 Units (250ml)

 A pint of cider on average is around 3.4 Units (6%)

 A pub shot of spirits is on average is around 1 Unit (25ml) (home measures are invariably larger)

 An alcopop is on average around 1.5 Units.

1 Unit	1 Unit	1 Unit	1 Unit	1 Unit	1 Unit
1 Unit	1 Unit	1 Unit	1 Unit	1 Unit	1 Unit
1 Unit	1 Unit	1 Unit	1 Unit	1 Unit	1 Unit
1 Unit	1 Unit	1 Unit	1 Unit	1 Unit	1 Unit
1 Unit	1 Unit	1 Unit	1 Unit	1 Unit	1 Unit

1 Unit	**1 Unit**	**1 Unit**	**1 Unit**	**1 Unit**	**1 Unit**
1 Unit	**1 Unit**	**1 Unit**	**1 Unit**	**1 Unit**	**1 Unit**
1 Unit	**1 Unit**	**1 Unit**	**1 Unit**	**1 Unit**	**1 Unit**
1 Unit	**1 Unit**	**1 Unit**	**1 Unit**	**1 Unit**	**1 Unit**
1 Unit	**1 Unit**	**1 Unit**	**1 Unit**	**1 Unit**	**1 Unit**
1 Unit	**1 Unit**	**1 Unit**	**1 Unit**	**1 Unit**	**1 Unit**
1 Unit	**1 Unit**	**1 Unit**	**1 Unit**	**1 Unit**	**1 Unit**
1 Unit	**1 Unit**	**1 Unit**	**1 Unit**	**1 Unit**	**1 Unit**

Exercise 3 – Out of Session Work

Ask the client to take the drink diary (on the worksheet below) home and monitor how much alcohol they use during the week. Ensure that you review the completed diary at the next session, and that the client actually completes the diary if this task is set. Otherwise, it may reinforce the notion that recording and monitoring the consumption of alcohol is irrelevant.

Exercise 3 – Out of Session Worksheet

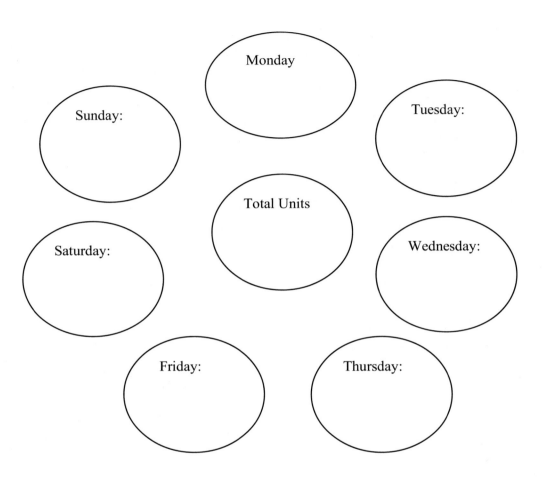

List all your reasons why you drink alcohol:

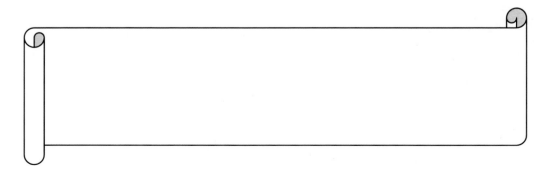

Circle the answer which best fits whom you drink with:

Monday: Alone / with others / bit of both

Tuesday: Alone / with others / bit of both

Wednesday: Alone / with others / bit of both

Thursday: Alone / with others / bit of both

Friday: Alone / with others / bit of both

Saturday: Alone / with others / bit of both

Sunday: Alone / with others / bit of both

Exercise 3 – Review

Name at least one thing that has been learned from this exercise.

Additional Notes:

Exercise 4 – Impact of Alcohol on Me

Category of exercise: Consequential thinking.

Tutor Notes

Understanding how alcohol impacts upon us is important. Generally, we know scientifically what happens, and this will be explored in the next exercise, but getting an understanding of how the client feels alcohol impacts on them will tell the facilitator a lot about the reasons why the client may use alcohol or how they perceive the implications of its use.

In this exercise, the facilitator should ask the client to consider their drinking in very general terms. Following this, the facilitator should present the client with the drinking blocks and ask the client how they feel this amount of alcohol affects them. With this exercise, the facilitator should point out that the client should start from the top and work downwards.

At the end of the exercise, the tutor should ask the client to consider two areas:

1. What does this exercise tell the client about their drinking?

2. What learning points can they take from the exercise?

The tutor should work with the client to fill out the answers to these questions at the bottom of the worksheet.

Step 1: Tell the client that this exercise considers their drinking in very general terms and is not looking at a specific incident.

Step 2: Show the client the worksheet with the drinking blocks and ask them to write inside the block how that volume of alcohol affects them.

Tip: Start from the top block and work in sequence downwards.

Step 3: At the end of the exercise, ask the client to consider the two questions below and discuss their answers with them:

1. What does this exercise tell the client about their drinking?

2. What learning points can they take from the exercise?

Tip: It is worth telling the offender that this exercise is not about demonstrating just how much they can 'handle' their drink – they have no reputation to maintain in this context. If they are resistant or struggle, then introduce humour to elicit some of the effects of alcohol; such as the phrase: "One tequila, two tequila, three tequila, floor."

Exercise 4 – Worksheet

Start here and work down >>

1 Alcoholic Drink

2 Alcoholic Drinks

3 Alcoholic Drinks

4 Alcoholic Drinks

5 Alcoholic Drinks

6 Alcoholic Drinks

7 Alcoholic Drinks

8 Alcoholic Drinks

9 Alcoholic Drinks

Exercise 4a – Alternative Exercise

This exercise is a great way to build rapport between a client and facilitator. It is also aimed at clients who are kinaesthetic learners and those who do not mind a bit of role play.

Step 1: Ask the client to stand up next to you - directly parallel. Next, tell the client that you are going to "pretend that we are both drinking alcohol." However, you (as facilitator) are only going to *mimic* the client's behaviours. This way the client can see (a bit like a mirror) what impact alcohol is having on them.

Step 2: Prompt the client by physically stepping forward and calling out the number of alcoholic drinks they have had at this point. Each physical step forward is one alcoholic drink. Ask the client to act out how they would behave if they had consumed that amount of alcohol. So for example:

Take one step forward, and say to the client: "One glass/pint of [insert drink of choice], what would you be doing?"

Step forward again, which is the second drink. Ask: "Act out how you would behave if you had two drinks."

Continue this up to 10 alcoholic drinks or when the offender gives the answer "passed out", whichever is most the most appropriate stage for the client.

Make sure that, as the facilitator, you are closely mimicking the client's behaviour. The idea is for the client to see how they look to others. If the client is being coy or modest, then over ape the actions.

Tip: Don't be afraid to make this exercise fun. It won't diminish the value of learning about the impact of drinking.

Step 3: Discuss with the client how they feel about 'seeing themselves' drunk and how/what other people may think when they see them acting in that manner. Try to elicit different emotions here (use the trigger triangle if it helps). Other people are not just going to see the behaviour as funny; they may feel fear, annoyance or anger. Explore the reasons for these different perspectives with the offender, again using the trigger triangle if necessary.

Exercise 4 – Out of Session Work

Should the facilitator feel that the client would benefit from further exploration and understanding into the impact of alcohol, and how this can be a very personal thing, this can be achieved by asking the client to undertake Exercise 4 with a friend or member of their family who also consumes alcohol, using the worksheet below.

Here, the client should follow all the same steps as they did in the exercise and discuss any differences or similarities in results with that person. In the next session that the facilitator has with the client, the client should then feedback their findings to the facilitator.

Exercise 4 – Out of Session Worksheet

Start here and
work down >>

1 Alcoholic Drink

2 Alcoholic Drinks

3 Alcoholic Drinks

4 Alcoholic Drinks

5 Alcoholic Drinks

6 Alcoholic Drinks

7 Alcoholic Drinks

8 Alcoholic Drinks

9 Alcoholic Drinks

Exercise 4 – Review

Name at least one thing that has been learned from this exercise.

Additional Notes:

Exercise 5 – Alcohol and General Health

Category of exercise: Consequential thinking.

Tutor notes

In this session, the facilitator will explore the general health implications that drinking alcohol to excess can have. Here the facilitator will need to explain that this information is based loosely on the information provided by the World Health Organisation (WHO).

Step 1: Prepare *two header cards*. These can simply be two pieces of A4 paper with *true* on one sheet, and *false* on the other. Additionally, cut out the statements on the worksheet below.

Step 2: Place the header cards on the table and, with the offender, read out the statements. Ask the client to identify if they consider the statements to be true or false.

For the tutor the answers are as follows:

True

Alcohol is a natural substance

Alcohol can kill you in large doses

Alcohol can lead to addiction

Alcohol can cause impotence.

Alcohol is a depressant

False

Alcohol is legal as it is less harmful than drugs

Alcohol is not linked with some liver problems

Alcohol cannot cause insomnia

Alcohol does not cause memory loss

Alcohol does not cause stomach disorders

Note: Additional empty cards are included for the facilitator to use for extra statements, should they want to.

Step 3: Without challenging the offender's answers, go through their reasoning for their choice of placement for each statement.

Step 4: Remove any statements that have been incorrectly placed on the header cards and move them to the bottom of the list of the correct header card. Discuss the changes with the offender and whether this challenges anything they believed previously.

Exercise 5 – Worksheet

Alcohol is a natural substance
Alcohol can kill you in large doses
Alcohol can lead to addiction
Alcohol can cause impotence.
Alcohol is a depressant
Alcohol is legal as it is less harmful than drugs.

Alcohol is not linked with some liver problems

Alcohol cannot cause insomnia

Alcohol does not cause memory loss

Alcohol does not cause stomach disorders

What have you learned from this exercise?

Exercise 5a – Alternative Exercise

At this stage, the aim is to identify the impact that alcohol can have on a *person*, rather than the impact it is having on the *client*. A narrow focus on the client at this stage could lead to justifications that alcohol use is not doing that much damage and would not increase awareness of the potential harm.

In this exercise the offender needs to complete the diagram of Max who is a dependant alcohol user.

Step 1: Read out (or read *with* the client) the case study of Max on the accompanying worksheet.

Step 2: Discuss briefly what health implications can be identified from the case study, and whether there are any more implication(s) categories, such as financial. If appropriate, the client can list their answers in the box provided on the worksheet, underneath the case study.

Step 3: Using the next worksheet, ask the offender to shade the health effects of alcohol with the correct colour according to the key. Then, shade the relevant parts on the person outline in the correct colours.

Exercise 5a – Worksheet

Case Study

Max is a 25 year old male who has been drinking alcohol daily for the last five years. Max has been on state benefits for the last two years as he has been signed off work for depression and concerns regarding his liver function. More recently, Max's doctor has referred him to the local hospital for biopsies as Max has reported continual diarrhoea and blood in his stools. The doctor has said that he is concerned Max may have the early stages of stomach or bowel cancer. Max feels as though he never has enough money and has thousands of pounds worth of debt. He gets £60 every week but spends £70 a week on alcohol. He does not recognise why he feels he never has enough money. Often, Max feels as though he has no support from anyone - but he refuses to leave the house or talk to anyone unless he has to go to the supermarket to buy alcohol.

List all the problems Max is having as a result of his alcohol use:

Health related

Other Categories/Problems

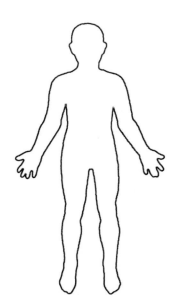

Key:

Head/brain – Red

Upper torso/heart –Blue

Lower torso/digestive system – Green

Heart disease

Increased risk of breast cancer

Dementia

Increased risk of stomach cancer

Irritable Bowel Syndrome

Depression

Reduced fertility

Liver disease

Pancreatitis

Problems with memory

Sickness and nausea

Diarrhoea

High blood pressure

Exercise 5 – Out of Session Work

Should the tutor view that the client would benefit from additional learning in this area, the tutor should ask the client to try to look up as many possible interesting facts about alcohol as possible with the focus being on health considerations. Provide the offender with the out of session worksheet to record any findings on.

Exercise 5 – Out of Session Worksheet

Fact	Source	Reliability

Exercise 5 – Review

Name at least one thing that has been learned from this exercise.

Additional Notes:

Exercise 6 – Impact of Alcohol on the Community

Category of exercise: Consequential thinking.

Tutor Notes

This exercise explores and aims to create a deeper understanding of how alcohol can impact on society. Here, rather than the facilitator relaying facts of alcohol, the emphasis is put on the client to consider how alcohol can impact on specific areas of life.

In order to complete this exercise, the facilitator should work through the worksheet with the client and consider how alcohol impacts on the areas identified. Answers should be encouraged from personal experiences as well as known facts.

Tip: Make sure that both the facilitator and the client differentiate and *discuss* the difference between experience, known scientific fact, and urban myth fact. The practitioner needs to be ready to challenge any incorrect urban myths.

Exercise 6 – Worksheet

What effects can alcohol have in the following areas? Be as diverse with your answers as possible:

Health

Behaviour (aggression)

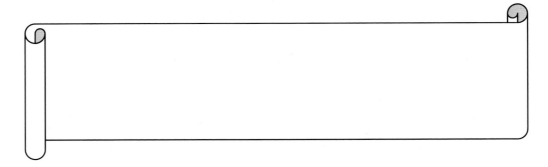

Relationships

Employment

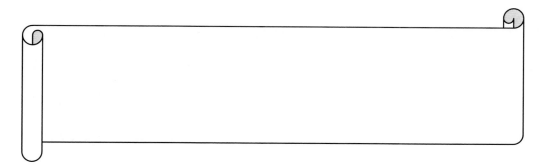

Finances

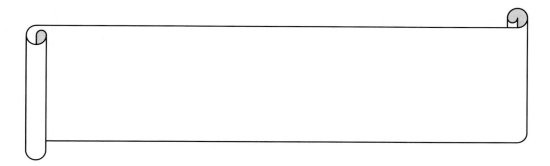

Looking at the effects of alcohol you have identified above, group them into the relevant categories below, depending on whom you think feels that effect:

Me

My friends

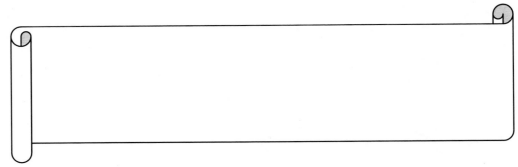

My family

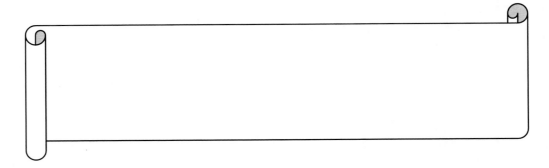

My acquaintances

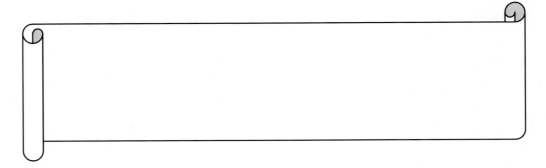

People in my local community

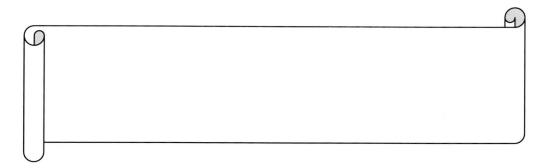

People in the wider community

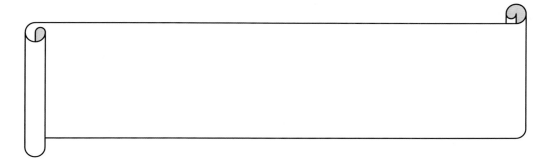

The government

'Society'

Exercise 6a – Alternative Exercise

This alternative exercise is a discussion-based exercise with key points being written down by the facilitator. A flip chart is ideal for this exercise. The facilitator, however, can also use a piece of A4 paper. There is some prior preparation involved.

Step 1: Cut out the 'money' on the accompanying worksheet.

Step 2: Ask the client to consider the following scenario: a 'drunken brawl' which starts in a pub and then spills out onto the road. At least one person is injured in the fight, and the Police are called by a resident of the local area who is scared by all the noise and violence. The Police radio for assistance from the ambulance service for the injured person. The fire brigade also have to be called out as one of the main antagonists saw the Police and tried to run away by vaulting a metal spiked fence; they slipped and impaled their leg on the spikes.

Step 3: Prompt the client to think about whom would be involved in the scenario, from the immediate incident and clear up, through to arrests and convictions. Write these on the flip chart sheet then lay the sheet on the floor.

Step 4: Give the client the 'money' and ask them to estimate how much each person identified on the flip chart would cost 'society' by placing the relevant amount by them. In order to assist here, consider the following questions.

1. Who would be involved? For example, Police, Prisons, Courts, staff to clean the mess up, the pub Landlord, local council, etc.

2. How much (at an estimate) would this cost society?

Use as an exact a figure as you can, based on the assumption that people involved will receive around £10 per hour.

Step 5: Add up the money for each person and total this by them. Discuss with the client as many different possible areas this money could be used, to help and support the community in a more positive way instead.

Exercise 6a – Worksheet

Exercise 6 – Out of Session Work

If the facilitator feels that the client should be encouraged to consider the wider cost of alcohol and how it can affect specific areas of life, the following out of session work may help.

Step 1: Run through the exercise prior to the end of the session and ensure that the client understands it.

Step 2: Tell the client to work out how much money they spent on their last four drinking sessions – this is then their 'budget'.

Step 3: With the aid of a shopping catalogue or online auction site, the client needs to create a 'wish list' or shopping list for the following people:

- Themselves
- Homeless person
- Single parent
- Child at Christmas time
- Pensioner on food shopping day

Step 4: At the next session, discuss the lists with the client in terms of the alternative value of their alcohol use.

Exercise 6 – Review

Name at least one thing that has been learned from this exercise.

Additional Notes:

Exercise 7 – Alcohol and More on Health

Category of exercise: Consequential thinking.

Tutor Notes

In this session, the facilitator will work with the client to consider more on how alcohol can impact on health, especially where the client considers themselves as having only a few 'harmless' drinks.

Step 1: The facilitator presents the client with prompts on the worksheet. These prompts are both visual prompts and verbal prompts.

Step 2: Allow the client time to consider the prompt; when they respond, the tutor should jot down underneath the prompt any thoughts and feelings that the client has.

Step 3: As part of each prompt, the facilitator should also examine what (if any) personal experiences the client has had in relation to the issues described in the worksheet.

Exercise 7 – Worksheet

Looking at the following facts about regular alcohol use, complete the following questions.

Alcohol can increase the likelihood of you suffering from depression.

What are your thoughts?

What are your feelings?

Have you got any personal experiences of this?

Alcohol use can increase the likelihood of developing heart disease.

What are your thoughts?

What are your feelings?

Have you got any personal experiences of this?

Alcohol use can increase the likelihood of brain damage.

What are your thoughts?

What are your feelings?

Have you got any personal experiences of this?

Alcohol use can increase the likelihood of liver disease.

What are your thoughts?

What are your feelings?

Have you got any personal experiences of this?

Alcohol use can increase the likelihood of weight gain.

What are your thoughts?

What are your feelings?

Have you got any personal experiences of this?

Alcohol use can increase the likelihood of disturbed sleep.

What are your thoughts?

What are your feelings?

Have you got any personal experiences of this?

Knowing the above facts, will this impact on you using alcohol in the future? If yes, how may it influence your usage? If no, why not?

Exercise 7a – Alternative Exercise

Tutor Notes

The invincibility of youth. The idea of this exercise is to compare what we/people think we know about alcohol, and what is actually true.

Step 1: Cut out the statements on the accompanying first worksheet (some will need to be sorted/removed according to the gender of the client).

Step 2: Provide the offender with the statements and the two outlines on the following worksheet. Ask them to place the statements around the outline wherever they think it applies. Outline 1 is the 'invincible' person, Outline 2 an average person.

Step 3: Go through the offender's choices with them; challenge and change any statements as appropriate.

Step 4: Ask the offender to consider which outline they most consider themselves to be like.

Step 5: If the offender picks the 'invincible' person, work with them to challenge their views of alcohol and its impact on their health. If they pick the 'average' person, work with them to look at their decision to continue using alcohol.

Exercise 7a – Worksheet (1)

Alcohol may give me a stomach ache but this is only temporary
Alcohol increases my likelihood of getting stomach cancer
Brewer's droop is made up by comedians
Alcohol damages the quality of my sperm
Alcohol affects my reproductive system and can increase side effects of the menopause
I just have a quick workout before a drinking session to keep a healthy balance
I know that drinking after a workout cancels out any of the benefits of that workout
I think that the odd duvet day off work to recover from a hangover never hurt anyone
I know that over 17 million working days are lost each year because of alcohol; this costs the economy a fortune
I'll never be one of the people in the statistics that die because of their alcohol use
I know that around 9000 people a year die because of their alcohol use
All I have to do is stop drinking and the negative effects will all go away

I know that the damage caused by alcohol can emerge years later
Alcohol won't affect my mental health – it makes me happy and lively
I know that alcohol is a depressant and can impact on memory if used heavily over a long period of time

Exercise 7a – Worksheet (2)

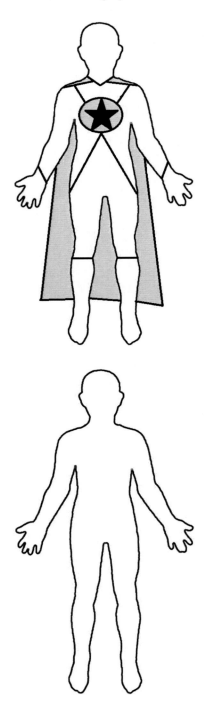

Exercise 7 – Out of Session Work

The facilitator should ask the client to do an investigation into the impact that alcohol has had on the life of friends or family members. To help, the client should be given the questionnaire on the worksheet to take away. Encourage the client to go for a range of ages and drinking styles; not all interviewees should be their fellow binge drinking friends, and so on. As always, review the answers with the client at the next session and challenge where appropriate.

Exercise 7 – Out of Session Worksheet

Use the following questions in your alcohol investigation.

1) Who are you interviewing?

2) What is their age?

3) How often do they drink alcohol? Do they think this is within or above the government guidelines?

4) What positives can they see from using alcohol?

5) What negatives can they see from using alcohol?

6) Do you have any observations about their answers? Would you have answered the questions differently, if you'd been doing the questionnaire for them? Why do you think this is?

Exercise 7 – Review

Name at least one thing that has been learned from this exercise.

Additional Notes:

Exercise 8 – Goal Setting

Category of exercise: General thinking skill.

Tutor notes

When it comes to alcohol misuse, it is important for the facilitator to consider with the client how to set realistic goals in relation to abstaining from, or reducing, alcohol use.

Here the facilitator should encourage the client to be specific about what their actual goal is. For example, is it to stop alcohol use completely or to reduce alcohol intake slowly?

Caution: Dependant alcoholics should not stop drinking alcohol quickly as this is dangerous and in some cases can be fatal. Ideally, they should seek support through their GP.

This exercise is in three parts.

Part 1

The facilitator should consider with the client whether their goal is to:

a) Stop drinking

b) Cut it down

This decision should be made by the client and not the facilitator as goal setting should be considered quite personal. However, the facilitator should encourage a discussion into this area and consideration should be given towards professional advice (e.g. a doctor) if that has been given.

To conclude the discussion, the facilitator should summarise what the broad goal is.

Part 2

The tutor should work through the subsequent worksheet with the client to consider if they are ready, willing, and able to change.

Part 3

The facilitator should consider the steps that the client needs to take to achieve their goal. But first, consider exactly what their goal is and if it is Specific, Measurable, Achievable, Realistic and Time bound. (SMART). The facilitator should encourage the client to be precise with their goal. Rather than stating:

"I want to cut my drinking down."

It would be better if the client was able to make a statement such as:

"I want to cut down my drinking by having one less pint of beer every day for the next week."

Once this goal has been set, place the goal at the top of the second worksheet and consider the steps needed to achieve this goal. Also, consider the obstacles identified in the first worksheet and how to overcome them, filling out the answers as appropriate.

Make sure the goal/steps are reviewed at appropriate points; in the example above the goal would need to be reviewed after one week. Once the set goal has been achieved, set another one and monitor this in the same manner as before. Keep this process going until the client is confident in their new behaviour. Subsequently, set reviews for longer periods of time to both check and support the long term continuation of the new behaviour.

Exercise 8 – Worksheet

The Ready, Willing and Able Questionnaire

1. Circle the statement which most suits you.

I want to stop drinking completely   *I want to cut down my drinking*

2. What is my reason for wanting to stop or cut down?

3. How important is it for you to achieve your goal?

4. Is there anything that could get in the way of you achieving your goal?

5. How will you overcome these obstacles?

If you are Ready, Willing, and Able - you can achieve your goal. Good luck!

Exercise 8 – Worksheet

My goal is:

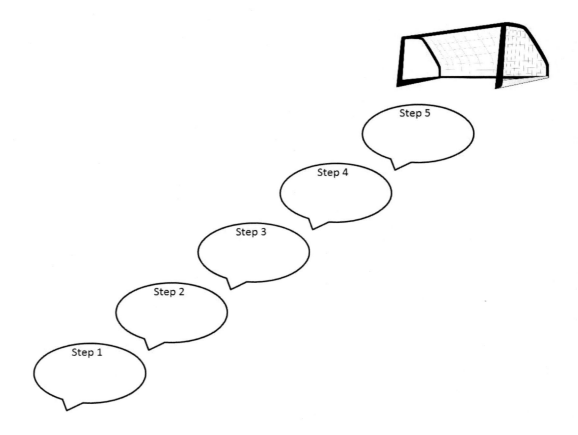

Exercise 8a – Alternative Exercise

The essence of Exercise 8 is the creation of a realistic and achievable path to a goal. This needs to be completed regardless of the learning style of the client. However, it may be that the manner in which the exercise is accomplished needs to be altered.

Utilising a brainstorming style of exercise, write 'Ready?' in one bubble, 'Willing?' in another, and 'Able?' in the third. Consider with the client what these terms mean and how they apply to them. Ask the client (where literacy allows) to take notes by expanding the bubbles. Here is an example of the 'Able' bubble.

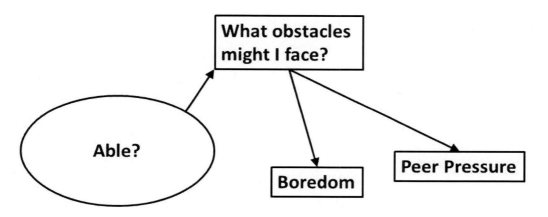

Tip: The facilitator can use Exercise 8's first worksheet as a prompt sheet for brainstorming each bubble.

Exercise 8a – Review

Name at least one thing that has been learned from this exercise.

Additional Notes:

Exercise 9 – Changing General Behaviour

Category of exercise: General thinking skill.

Tutor notes
Behaviour Skills. Here, the facilitator will consider with the client useful ways in which the client can manage, or prevent, their alcohol use depending on the client's goal (i.e. stop versus reduce consumption).

Step 1: Consider, with the client, all the reasons why the client uses alcohol. List the reasons in the relevant worksheet space. Examples such as: 'relaxing' and 'confidence' may be relevant here.

Step 2: Ask the client to consider alternative behaviours which they do/have done/could do instead of drinking. Treat this very much as a 'brainstorming' exercise; at this stage, the answers do not need to link to the answers given in Step 1.

Tip: If the client struggles to think of alternative behaviours, simply ask them to think of any behaviour they enjoy which is not related to alcohol. If they still struggle to remove alcohol from the scenario, ask them to think about a time in their lives before alcohol and build suggestions from that.

Step 3: Transfer the answers from Step 1 into the first column of the worksheet below.

Step 4: Ask the client to take their suggestions from Step 2 and place them into the second column alongside *relevant* items in the first column. Relevant means behaviours which the client believes *they* could successfully use to replace their alcohol dependent behaviour. The client can obviously add more suggestions if they think of them.

For example:

Reason for using alcohol	Alternative suggestion
Gives me confidence	Go out with a friend I feel comfortable with Speak to GP about counselling to improve self-image Join a tennis club as I used to be good at tennis

Exercise 9 – Worksheet

Reasons why I
use alcohol

Alternative
behaviours to
drinking alcohol

Exercise 9 – Worksheet 2

Reason for using alcohol	Alternative suggestion

Exercise 9a – Alternative Exercise

This exercise requires the practitioner to have prior knowledge of the client and possible activities in the local area. It also requires some prior preparation.

Step 1: Complete as many of the cards as possible on the worksheet below by writing down reasons the client uses alcohol (use assessments made of the client) and other non-alcohol dependant and available activities in the area (or which the client is known to enjoy).

Tip: Try to keep the 'reasons' cards in equal numbers to the 'alternatives' cards.

Step 2: With the client, ask them if they can think of any reasons why they use alcohol, and activities they could do instead of drinking. If the client thinks of any additional reasons or activities (to those from step 1) add them to the cards.

Step 3: Play pairs with the cards; make two piles of cards: one of reasons to drink and the other of alternative activities. Spread out each pile face down on the table but maintaining two distinct areas. Turn over two cards at a time, one from each pile/area. Ask the offender to read out the two cards as a statement: 'One of the reasons I drink is … and an alternative could be …'

Step 4: If the client agrees with the statement they have read out take the cards out of the area of play and leave them together, face up, above the 'game'.

Step 5: Once all possible pairings have been made, remove any cards which are still face down. Transfer the information on the pairs to the worksheet and discuss with the client their views about putting these alternatives into place.

Exercise 9a – Worksheet

Exercise 9 – Out of Session Work

There are alternatives to drinking around us all the time; all it takes is a willingness to both see and try them.

Step 1: Between sessions, ask the client to keep a watch out for people not using alcohol. This can be either in their day to day life, or on television, or even in discussion with friends.

Step 2: For every example they come across, ask the client to complete a row on the worksheet below.

For example:

Alternative activity identified	Details – where, how, when, etc.	Would I consider trying this? Reasons…	I have now tried this and the results were…
Drinking cola	At the pub in the day, instead of beer	Yes, in the day time - It may stop me getting too drunk too quickly	Worked the first time with my workmates but not with my old college mates

Step 3: At the next session review the completed worksheet and discuss, challenge, and encourage the answers as appropriate.

Exercise 9 – Out of Session Worksheet

Alternative activity identified	Details – where, how, when, etc.	Would I consider trying this? Reasons…	I have now tried this and the results were…

Exercise 9 – Review

Name at least one thing that has been learned from this exercise.

Additional Notes:

Exercise 10 – Dodge, Deal, Divert (DDD)

Category of exercise: General thinking skill.

Tutor Notes

This is a strategy commonly used in accredited programmes. It helps offenders consider what to do in a difficult situation; they can either Dodge the situation, Deal with the situation, or Divert the situation (DDD).

Step 1: Explain to the client that, in any given situation, anyone can control or tackle their own behaviour by either: Dodging the situation that triggered it, Dealing with the situation, or Diverting the situation.

Remember: we cannot control everything that happens to us, but we can control how we behave in response!

Step 2: Discuss matters with the client by asking them their opinions on the above statement. Here, you are only looking to try to understand the offender's stance on the topic and then extrapolating possible examples of when they walked away from something, confronted a situation, or avoided it completely. You could ask the offender questions along the lines of: "Tell me an example of when you have not controlled something that has happened to you?"

Step 3: Write the words Dodge, Deal and Divert on the top of the worksheet.

Step 4: Ask the client to think about as many different practical ways in which they could have Dodged, Dealt with, or Diverted from the situation which led to their offending behaviour or the situation they gave as an example in Step 2.

Step 5: Highlight with the client that they can use this strategy whenever they recognise themselves to be in a difficult situation.

Step 6: The practitioner can ask the client which strategies under each heading they are most likely to use, then writes them on a small piece of card - no bigger than a business card you may find in your wallet. Then the practitioner tells the client: "Should you recognise that you are in a difficult situation, just pull out your DDD card and look at ways to handle the situation."

Exercise 10 – Worksheet

Dodge	Deal	Divert

Cut out the following card:

DDD Card

Dodge:

Deal:

Divert:

For more information, email:
interventioninfo@ymail.com

Exercise 10a – Alternative Exercise

The idea of this exercise is to provide the offender with strategies to avoid and cope with risk situations, but also to increase their acceptance towards alternative strategies.

Step 1: Read the three scenarios on the worksheet below to the offender. Ask them to consider at least one *other* way in which the person concerned could have handled the situation. Note this suggestion in the top box below the scenario.

Step 2: Once all the scenarios have been read and annotated. Explain to the offender that there are three ways of managing a situation – dodging it, dealing with it, and diverting from it. Ask them to consider whether their suggestion fitted in to: dodge, deal, or divert.

Tip: If the offender has picked one category for all their answers, discuss why they think this may be, and whether they routinely use this in their own life. For example, if all of their suggestions were to 'dodge', does this link to their use of alcohol as a 'dodging' of problems?

Step 3: With the offender, find other alternative behaviours to each scenario so that the offender would be able to *pick* from dodge, deal or divert strategies. Note the additional two strategies in the other two boxes below each scenario.

Step 4: Ask the offender to consider either their offence or a specific problematic situation related to their alcohol use and write this in the space provided after the scenarios. Then ask the offender to consider three different ways in which they could have managed this situation, one for each of dodge, deal, and divert.

Tip: It is always worth briefly discussing with the offender why they did not choose an alternative behaviour; even if the answer to that question is simply that they 'hadn't thought about it'.

Exercise 10a – Worksheet

Scenario 1

Ben was in his local pub when he saw a person he did not recognise at the bar. Ben thought that he saw this person looking at him but when he looked he was not able to make eye contact. Throughout the evening, a few of Ben's friends said that they also thought this person was looking at him. Eventually, towards the end of the night, Ben decided to confront the person at the bar. This confrontation ended in an altercation and Ben hit the person with a bottle.

| |
| |
| |

Scenario 2

Amy was at a friend's house watching a DVD. The friend suggested that they order a pizza and drink some wine. Once the wine bottle was finished, they both wanted more. The friend suggested breaking into her flatmate's room to see if she had any. Amy felt uncomfortable at the suggestion but said nothing. They both broke in and took a couple of bottles. The following day, the flatmate returned home and said that some pieces of jewellery were missing from her room; she reported the theft to the Police. Eventually Amy was arrested and charged with theft.

| |
| |
| |

Scenario 3

Steve was out in town with friends drinking, they were having a great time until they realised that they'd missed the last train home. One of the friends Steve was with had driven to town with the intention of getting the train home and collecting his car in the morning. As they'd missed the train, they all decided that it would be okay to drive back with this friend as he'd drunk the least throughout the evening. On the way home, the friend lost control of the car and crashed. One of the group was killed in the collision and Steve broke his leg which resulted in him losing his temporary employment.

My offending/problematic situation:

Three different ways I could have managed this:

Exercise 10 – Out of Session Work

The facilitator asks the client to list all the situations they have encountered (if any) over the post-session week where they have dodged, dealt with, or diverted from situations where they were tempted to use alcohol. For this exercise, the tutor should give the client the Out of Session Worksheet. The last column on the worksheet can be completed by the offender out of session if they wish but must be reviewed within a session with the practitioner.

Exercise 10 – Out of Session Worksheet

List all the times when you have Dodged, Dealt with, or Diverted from situations where you were tempted to use alcohol.

Situation	When and Where	Skill used	Reflections on effectiveness

Exercise 10 – Review

Name at least one thing that has been learned from this exercise.

Additional Notes:

Exercise 11 – High Risk Situations

Category of exercise: General thinking skill.

Tutor Notes

Even where a client is motivated (ready, willing, and able – see Exercise 8) within a session, they will still have to face their regular day to day environment. This will present the client with temptations to revert to previous behaviours. The more tempting these situations, the greater the risk that the client will abandon their goals.

In this session, the facilitator will consider with the client some possible situations that the client will need to gain control over - when the client is at their highest risk of using alcohol. These are known as *high risk situations*.

By discussing high risk situations and potential strategies for managing them, the practitioner is not attempting to dissuade the client from attempting change, or indeed being pessimistic about their likelihood of success. It is in fact quite the opposite, by giving the client as much information about the challenges they will face and addressing them in a supportive environment, the client is given the best possible chance of success.

This exercise ideally follows Exercise 10 so that the client has some idea of different strategies they could use to manage risk situations.

Step 1: Consider the following three areas with the client:

- Who they use alcohol with
- Where they tend to use alcohol
- When they tend to use alcohol

Step 2: Write the client's answers to these areas in the relevant part of the worksheet.

Step 3: Consider with the client whether the best strategy to manage each risk area would be avoid (dodge), cope (deal) or escape (divert). Then note *how* they would implement this strategy. Complete the summary sentences at the end of the worksheet.

Step 4: Review the success of these strategies at subsequent sessions when the client has had the opportunity to test them out.

Exercise 11 – Worksheet

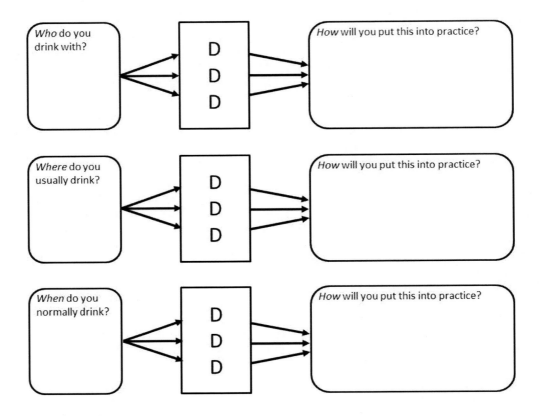

My high risk situations are:

I will manage these by:

Exercise 11a – Alternative Exercise

This exercise is for the more visual learner. The principles of the exercise are the same as for DDD - but it is presented in a less 'wordy' illustrated form.

Step 1: Ask the client to consider what they think their most high risk situation would be. As prompts, discuss who they drink with, when they tend to drink, and where they tend to drink. Write the client's answer at the top of the worksheet.

Step 2: Explain that one way to envisage alcohol use is by seeing our urge, or need to use, as a form of attack from the alcohol. If this is the case, then our motivation not to use needs to build a defensive wall. This defensive wall consists of ideas and strategies against alcohol use.

Step 3: Using the DDD method from Exercise 10, consider different strategies to manage the identified high risk situation and note each one on a layer of bricks on the wall on the worksheet. The more ideas the client can find, the more defensive their wall.

Exercise 11a – Worksheet

When do you think you are most likely to drink alcohol?

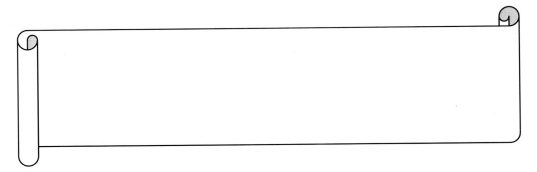

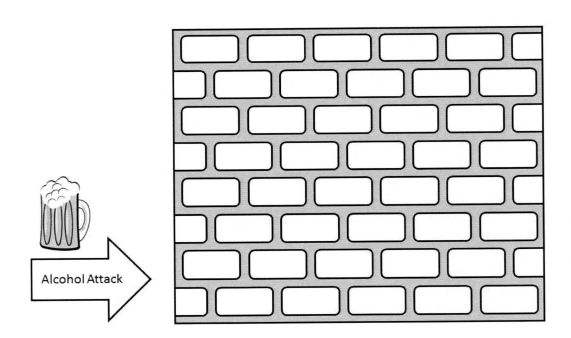

Alcohol Attack

Exercise 11 – Out of Session Work

If the client struggles to complete the worksheet, then the facilitator should ask the client to record (using the questionnaire below) when, with who, and where they consume alcohol over the following week. Here, the facilitator should explain to the client that they do not need to provide just one answer for all the questions. Use the completed worksheet from this Out of Session work to assist in completing Exercise 11's primary worksheet at the next session.

In order to gain a defence against old alcohol related behaviours, the client needs to be open to new ideas and ways of managing risk situations.

Step 1: Ask the client to consider a 'superhero' who is invulnerable to the negative influences of alcohol. They need to find a name for this superhero and write this on the worksheet.

Step 2: This superhero is able to utilise any strategy to manage risk situations, no matter how wacky. The client needs to think of as many different possible strategies for their superhero, and note them on the worksheet around the character.

Step 3: At the following session, review all the strategies the client has thought of and discuss with them how practical they are in real life, whether they could be adapted to become realistic, and whether the client would (or could) use them for themselves.

Exercise 11 – Out of Session Worksheet

Who do you use alcohol with?

When do you use alcohol? (times of day/particular events/different emotional states and so on)

Where do you tend to drink alcohol?

What do you feel your high risk (times you are most likely to use alcohol) situations are?

What ideas can you think of to try and manage a high risk situation successfully?

Superhero name - _____

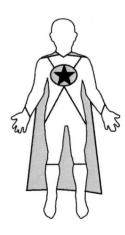

Exercise 11 – Review

Name at least one thing that has been learned from this exercise.

Additional Notes:

Exercise 12 – Final Exercise

Category of exercise: General thinking skill.

Tutor Notes

In this session, the facilitator is encouraged to discuss with the client where the client can go to for support, and when they should use this support.

Step 1: Consider who the client 'thinks of' as support. List these on the worksheet.

Step 2: Only when the client has finished listing all the relevant people or organisations they can think of should the facilitator suggest other support networks which may be appropriate. An example could be, if relevant, their Probation Officer or Housing Support Officer.

Tip: As facilitator, take note of who the client thinks of as support in this area. This may require gentle challenging on the part of the facilitator if the support proposed by the client is not appropriate. To simply present a list of organisations to a client may shut them down. If it was that easy, they would have contacted an organisation previously!

Step 3: Following the completion of the support grid, the client should consider all the learning points they have taken from each session and list them in the subsequent worksheet.

Note: Whilst the practitioner may wish to have a copy of this exercise for the client's records, it is imperative that the client takes the master copy!

Exercise 12 – The Worksheet

My Support Network

Name	Type of Support	Telephone Number	Address	When Can I Contact Them?
AA	Emergency Helpline	0845 769 7555	N/a	In a Crisis

Exercise 12 – Review

Write down what you have learned from the exercises in this workbook.

1.

2.

3.

4.

5.

6.

7.

8.

9.

10.

11.

12.

Useful Numbers and websites for addressing alcohol misuse

Organisation	Contact Details
Alcoholics Anonymous	www.alcoholics-anonymous.org.uk 0845 769 7555
SMART Recovery	www.smartrecovery.org.uk
NHS Choices	www.nhs.uk/livewell/alcohol
Drink Aware	www.drinkaware.co.uk
Add your own information here	